SOUTH AFRICA

A Tapestry of Peoples and Traditions

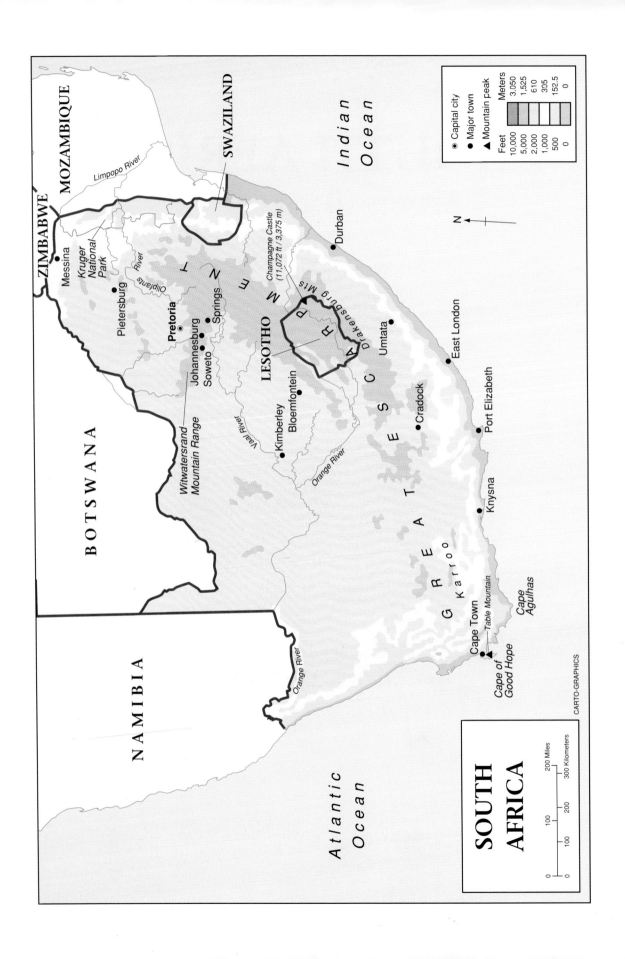

SOUTH AFRICA

MOZAMBIQUE

SWAZILAND

ZIMBABWE

Indian Ocean

Limpopo River

Messina

Kruger National Park

Oliphants River

Durban

Champagne Castle (11,072 ft / 3,375 m)

Pietersburg

Springs

Pretoria

Johannesburg

Soweto

LESOTHO

Drakensburg Mts

East London

Umtata

BOTSWANA

Witwatersrand Mountain Range

Kimberley

Bloemfontein

Cradock

Port Elizabeth

Vaal River

Orange River

G R E A T E S C A R P

Knysna

NAMIBIA

Orange River

Cape Town

Table Mountain

Karroo

Cape Agulhas

Cape of Good Hope

CARTO-GRAPHICS

Atlantic Ocean

N

Capital city
Major town
▲ Mountain peak

Feet	Meters
10,000	3,050
5,000	1,525
2,000	610
1,000	305
500	152.5
0	0

0 — 100 — 200 Miles

0 — 100 — 200 — 300 Kilometers

SOUTH AFRICA

A Tapestry of Peoples and Traditions

Jacqueline Drobis Meisel

BENCHMARK **B**OOKS

MARSHALL CAVENDISH
NEW YORK

With thanks to Deborah Kaspin, Assistant Professor of Anthropology at Yale University, for her expert review of the manuscript.

WITH LOVE ALWAYS, TO ALEX, MATTHEW, AND JOSHUA.

Benchmark Books
Marshall Cavendish Corporation
99 White Plains Road
Tarrytown, New York 10591-9001

© Marshall Cavendish Corporation 1997

Library of Congress Cataloging-in-Publication Data
Meisel, Jacqueline Drobis.
    South Africa : a tapestry of peoples and traditions / Jacqueline Drobis Meisel.
        p.   cm. — (Exploring cultures of the world)
    Includes bibliographical references (p.   ) and index.
    Summary: Discusses the geography, history, people, cultural life, and education of the various ethnic groups making up the South African nation.
    ISBN 0-7614-0335-3
    1. South Africa—Juvenile literature. [1. South Africa.] I. Title. II. Series.
DT1719.M45   1997
968—dc20   96-18997
                                                                        CIP
                                                                        AC

Printed in Hong Kong
Series design by Carol Matsuyama

Front cover: A Zulu man and his son in ceremonial dress.
Back cover: Children play at an integrated playground in Durban.

Photo Credits
Front cover, title page, and pages 10, 20, 26–27: ©Steve Vidler/Leo de Wys, Inc.; back cover and pages 22, 23, 25, 30, 34, 39, 41, 42, 47, 53, 55: ©Alex Meisel; page 6: ©Ken Oosterbroek/Gamma Liaison; pages 12, 15, 45: ©Bob Krist/Leo de Wys, Inc.; page 16: North Wind Picture Archives; page 19: ©Impact Visuals/Kuninori Takahashi/PNI; pages 29, 33: ©Black Star/Selwyn Tait/PNI; page 37: ©Black Star/Joao Silver/PNI; pages 38, 48, 49: ©Jason Lauré; page 50: ©Peter Magubane/Gamma Liaison; page 52: ©South Light/Frankenfeld/Gamma Liaison; page 54: ©Alon Reininger/Leo de Wys, Inc.; page 56: ©Ulf Andersen/Gamma Liaison

Contents

Nelson Mandela campaigning to become South Africa's first black president

1

GEOGRAPHY AND HISTORY

The Land Where Two Oceans Meet

No Easy Walk to Freedom

Nelson Rolihlahla Mandela was born in 1918 in the Umtata district of South Africa. He grew up to become the world's most famous political prisoner. He is a symbol of the struggle for racial equality. Mandela became South Africa's first black president in 1994.

As a young boy, he lived with his family in a kraal (CRAWL), or homestead. The kraal is a cluster of huts surrounding a pen for cattle. His father was a chief who had four wives. Nelson's mother, Nosekeni, had three daughters after Nelson was born.

Nelson was nine years old when his father died. His close relative Chief Jongintaba (yong-in-TAH-bah), took charge of him. Jongintaba made sure that Nelson received an excellent education from elementary school through university.

Mandela gave up his right to take his father's place as chief when he decided to go to law school. As a university student, he met other students of all races and learned many new ideas. Coming from a rural African way of life, he found the activity in the city of

Johannesburg exciting. Mandela decided he could no longer accept the harsh, unfair treatment of his fellow black South Africans, and he joined the African National Congress (ANC) in 1944. He helped form the organization's Youth League. In addition, he and a friend set up South Africa's first black law partnership.

In 1948, the South African government began its policy of apartheid (uh-PAR-tate). This was a system of racial segregation, or separation. The ANC called for equality for all races and began challenging the government. In 1952, Mandela led the Defiance of Unjust Laws Campaign and was taken into custody for a few days, then released.

In 1956, Mandela, along with 155 other people, was charged with "treason and other serious crimes" against the government but was found not guilty. In 1958, he married Winnie Madikizela, who fought alongside her husband in the struggle against apartheid.

The government outlawed the ANC in 1960, but Mandela continued its work and went into hiding. He helped create a group called Umkhonto we Sizwe (oom-KON-to weh SEEZ-weh), or Spear of the Nation, to try to force change.

For his actions, Mandela was arrested in 1962, convicted, and later sentenced to life in prison. While in jail, growing anti-apartheid forces inside and outside of South Africa argued that he should be freed. In the 1980s, people around the world became aware of his situation. The popular song "Free Nelson Mandela" was played on radio stations all over the world. However, in South Africa, people were not allowed to read his books and articles. As time went on, more and more people believed that Mandela was a wise man. They thought he might be able to help his country's black people become free in a peaceful way.

Shortly before Mandela's release from prison in 1990, the South African government made the ANC a legal group once again. After his release, Mandela worked toward peace with South African president F. W. de Klerk and other government leaders. In 1990 and 1991, the government did away with apartheid. And in 1993, Nelson Mandela and de Klerk were awarded the Nobel Peace Prize. The first elections in which people of all races could vote were held in April 1994 and Nelson Mandela was elected president.

The Southernmost Tip of Africa

South Africa sits at the southernmost tip of Africa. To the northwest is Namibia. To South Africa's north is Botswana. Toward the northeast are Zimbabwe and Mozambique. South Africa's eastern boundary is the Indian Ocean, and to the south and west is the Atlantic Ocean.

The tiny independent country of Lesotho lies entirely within South Africa, and the small kingdom of Swaziland is almost completely surrounded by South Africa.

Misty Mountains and Bushveld

South Africa is a country of many different kinds of awesome beauty. There are areas of rain forest, sweeping veld (grasslands), rugged mountain ranges, and deserts.

The Highveld is a huge flat area that takes up a big part of the center of the country. It lies between 4,000 and 6,000 feet (1,219 to 1,829 meters) above sea level. This area of grasslands is bordered by a mountain range that is called the Witwatersrand Ridge. The Witwatersrand is well known for its rich gold deposits.

The Middleveld in the northwest supports many farms. The Lowveld in the southeast lies at sea level. Among its tall grasses and scattered shrubs, baboons, monkeys, and duikers (small antelope) can be found.

Rich farmland is surrounded by a mountain range in the northwestern part of South Africa.

The Great Escarpment is a series of cliffs and mountains that separates the veld from the eastern coastal plain. It reaches its tallest heights in the Drakensberg Mountains that soar up in the east between the Highveld and the Lowveld.

Along the Indian Ocean coastline stand dense tropical rain forests. A hundred years ago parts of this forest were cleared to make way for the endlessly rolling hills of sugar-cane plantations. Inland, toward Swaziland, the land changes and pine forests rise up in the hills. Much of the western portion of South Africa is a desert called the Karroo, meaning "land of thirst."

South Africa's interior receives little rainfall, so there are no big freshwater lakes. Only two large rivers, the Orange (and its tributary, or branch, the Vaal) and the Limpopo, run through the land. The Orange River flows west from its source in Lesotho to the Atlantic Ocean. The Limpopo River begins near Johannesburg and winds across eastern South Africa and Mozambique to the Indian Ocean. But neither river is deep enough to carry large ships.

A Land Rich in Resources

Temperatures in South Africa vary depending on altitude. On some high mountains, the peaks are snow covered year-round. Hot, humid weather is likely to be found at sea level along the northeastern coast. Much of the country, however, enjoys a mild, sunny climate most of the year. Since South Africa lies in the Southern Hemisphere, its winter begins in May and ends in September.

Even though South Africa's climate is fairly dry, the country has a wonderful variety of plants and animals. Many species of wildlife roam freely in rural areas. Large wild animals, including elephants, lions, zebra, wildebeest, giraffes, and rhinoceroses, live in natural surroundings in ten major national game parks. A game park is a reserve for wildlife. The largest is Kruger National Park. It is about the size of the state of Massachusetts! Visitors can drive slowly through and spot animals in their natural habitat. An incredibly long, strong

Visitors to the Mala Mala Game Reserve in the northern part of South Africa can see wild animals in their natural habitats.

fence encloses Kruger National Park. The fence keeps animals safe inside the park. It also keeps out poachers—people who hunt animals illegally.

The trees and plants vary greatly from region to region depending on such factors as temperature, altitude, and rainfall. In the eastern Lowveld, where it rains a lot, lush tropical palm, papaya, and banana trees grow. Ancient forests of yellowwood, ironwood, and cedar stand here, too. In areas where rainfall is lighter, such as in flat open grassland, about 350 different kinds of low shrubs grow. Some of the plants, such as aloe, are used for medicines. Vegetation, however, is sparse in the rocky and dry Karroo Desert. Once a year, though, rains cause the desert to come alive in a blaze of colorful flowers.

Underground in South Africa, enormous mineral deposits can be found. In fact, South Africa produces almost two thirds of the world's gold and more than one quarter of its diamonds. Coal, iron, platinum, copper, and uranium are also mined in great quantities. The only major natural resource that South Africa does *not* have is oil.

The First Inhabitants

Many thousands of years ago, much of southern Africa, including present-day South Africa, was inhabited by people called the San. They lived in small groups and were hunter-gatherers—they both hunted animals and gathered plants for food. Then, about 2,000 years ago, sheep, goat, and cattle herders related to the San, appeared. These herders were the Khoikhoi (KOY-KOY), or Khoi.

The peaceful way of life of the San and the Khoi was eventually disturbed by people who moved down from central Africa around A.D. 300. These people, who spoke the language called Bantu (BAHN-tu), were the ancestors of today's black South Africans. Farmers and cattle tenders, they used iron to make tools and weapons. They conquered the San and Khoi who lay in their path on their way south and east. Over time, they formed kingdoms and supported themselves by herding livestock and growing cereal grains.

Europeans Arrive

In the 1400s, Portuguese traders sailed around the tip of southern Africa in search of a route to the East, where they would buy spices to sell back home. Some of these sailors stopped at the Cape of Good Hope—a perfect place to rest and find food for the long journey to Asia. The Khoi and the San, brown-skinned peoples, were shocked to see that the sailors had white skin.

Eventually, as Portugal grew less powerful, English and Dutch trading ships competed to gain control of this valuable spice route that went around the tip of Africa.

The people who worked for Holland's Dutch East India Company were the first Europeans to settle in South Africa. In 1652, the company sent Jan van Riebeeck to set up a refreshment station. This would make it easier for the ships to get fresh food and water on their way to Asia. The little refreshment station grew into a village, then a town, and finally a Dutch colony called Cape Town.

As their numbers grew, the settlers took more and more land from the native people. Conflicts erupted, but the Dutch had superior weapons. Many Khoi moved away from this area into the interior of the country. Some who chose to remain became paid servants.

As the size of the colony grew, German and French immigrants joined the Dutch settlers at the Cape. Many of these immigrants came to be known first as Boers (BOORS), from the Dutch word for farmers, then as Afrikaners—the white tribe.

In 1814, the British took over the Cape colony from the Dutch. The British recognized the Cape's strategic importance in trading with the East. It was a good refueling stop on the way to India. At first, they introduced laws for the better treatment of slaves and free "coloreds." *Colored* was the term used

The Cape of Good Hope is Africa's southernmost point. In 1488, European sailors stopped to rest nearby before continuing on their voyage to Asia.

by the Europeans for people of mixed race. Later, in 1833, the British outlawed slavery completely.

The Boers hated the way that the British tried to tell them what they could and could not do. Thousands of Boers packed up their belongings and moved into the interior of the country to get away from British control. They traveled through unknown territory by ox wagons on their journey, known as the Great Trek. They were often called *trekboers* (TREK-boors), or "farmers on the move." The *trekboers* often met the Bantu-speaking Xhosa (KHO-zah) people and competed with them for the same grazing land. They fought small battles as well as

A Boer farm

full-scale frontier wars for territory. By the early 1850s, two independent Boer republics were created—the Transvaal and the Orange Free State.

Diamonds and Gold

Around this time, diamonds and gold were discovered in the Boer republics. Many fortune hunters came into the area, and they began mining operations. The British wanted to take over the Boer republics so that they could have the gold and diamond fields for themselves. This led to a war between the English and the Boers called the Anglo-Boer War. The war began in 1899. It ended in 1902 with the Boers' surrender to the British.

In 1910, the two Boer republics and the two British colonies—the Cape and Natal—joined together to form the Union of South Africa. These areas became the four provinces that made up South Africa. (In 1994, the new government reorganized the country into nine provinces.) The country was given self-government within the British Empire. South Africa grew rich because there were many black people who worked for low pay in the mines, on farms, and in industry. White people saved all the best jobs for themselves. Most black people were poor, while most white people lived comfortably.

From Apartheid to Democracy

People of different races had been kept apart, or segregated, in South Africa for many years. Starting in 1948, however, strict laws were made to make sure that the races didn't mix. This was the beginning of the system of apartheid. People were classified as white, black, colored, or Asian. (Sometimes Asians were referred to as Indians.) There were laws about

SOUTH AFRICAN GOVERNMENT

In 1994, a new form of government in South Africa replaced the old system of apartheid. The Republic of South Africa has a Cabinet and a Parliament, and nine provincial governments. The Cabinet consists of the president—Nelson Mandela—two deputy presidents, and twenty-seven Cabinet ministers. Parliament is made up of the National Assembly and the Senate.

South Africa has three government capitals. The administrative capital is in Pretoria. The legislative, or law-making, capital is in Cape Town. The judicial capital is in Bloemfontein.

A new Constitution was written in 1994. It guarantees the elimination of apartheid and includes a Bill of Fundamental Rights. This provides equal treatment under the law for everyone, regardless of race, color, religion, or sex.

where a person could live depending on his or her race. People who were not white had to carry a special identity book, called a Pass Book, to show where they lived and worked. They needed permission in order to travel. Schools, hospitals, public transportation, and recreational facilities such as swimming pools, beaches, and playgrounds were all segregated. Education for whites was superior to that provided for the other groups, and only white people were allowed to vote.

Many people who protested against the unfairness of this system were put in prison. One of the most famous political prisoners was Nelson Mandela. He was part of a group that tried to end apartheid. He was arrested in 1962 and spent twenty-eight years in prison. The white government set him free in 1990 when it began to realize that a civil war might break out if it did not end apartheid. In the early 1990s, Mandela and other political leaders of all races held many meetings to try to figure out a peaceful way to end apartheid. It was very difficult, but at last, in April 1994, the first democratic elections were held in South Africa. For the first time, every citizen of every race over age eighteen could vote. Mandela himself became the president.

South African women celebrate their party's entry into the 1994 elections.

Zulu children dress in ceremonial costumes for a festival.

2
THE PEOPLE

The South African Way

South Africa has almost 45 million people from many different racial and ethnic groups. They speak dozens of different languages and practice a variety of customs and religions.

Black South Africans

Black South Africans, also referred to as Africans, are descended from many tribes, or ethnic groups. The largest groups of people are Zulu, Xhosa, and Sotho.

Most Zulu (ZOO-loo) people live in Kwazulu-Natal, the new name of the province of Natal. Before the British conquest, the Zulu were farmers and cattle herders. They traditionally practiced polygamy, the custom in which a man has more than one wife at the same time. A traditional Zulu family consisted of a man, his wives, his unmarried children, and his married sons and their wives and children. Today, polygamy is less common in cities and towns, and most families are smaller in size.

Many Zulu people, such as this boy and young man, still live in much the same manner as their ancestors did.

The Xhosa (KHO-zah) people are South Africa's second-largest culture group, after the Zulus. In the old days, before the Xhosa people left their traditional territory to work in the cities, they were a rural people who raised crops and kept cattle. Now, however, more than half the Xhosa live away from their original homes, mainly in mining areas.

The Sotho (SUE-too) people come from the high grassland areas of southern Africa. Traditionally they cultivated crops and kept animals. They grew corn, millet, beans, and sweet potatoes. Since the time that gold and diamonds were discovered in South Africa, the majority of the Sotho have left the rural areas to find work and live in Johannesburg and other cities. It is still possible, however, to see their tiny villages of circular huts with thatched roofs.

Colored South Africans

The people defined in South Africa as colored are a blend of white-, brown-, and black-skinned people. They are the mixed descendants of the Khoi, the San, and other southern African peoples. Under apartheid, this group was discriminated against. In that system, although coloreds were better off than blacks, they were still regarded as far below whites.

Asian South Africans

There are more than 1.5 million Asians in South Africa. Approximately 12,000 of them are of Chinese origin. Most South African Asians, however, are of Indian descent. People from India were first brought to South Africa in the 1860s to work on sugarcane plantations. After their contracts expired, they could choose to stay or return to India. Many who stayed became market gardeners, people who sold produce from carts on the street. Others became traders. Many of these opened businesses in the city of Durban, which is more than half Asian.

An Indian merchant sells spices, such as curry, in her shop.

One of the best-known Indians who lived in South Africa for many years was Mahatma Gandhi. Between the years 1906 and 1914, he led the *Satyagraha*, which was a non-violent campaign against racial discrimination. Gandhi later became a great leader in India. Today, most of South Africa's Indians live in the province Kwazulu-Natal. Most speak English, although some still speak Indian languages.

Most Indians are either Hindu or Muslim. Some Muslim men wear long tunics over their trousers and crocheted skull-caps on their heads in observance of the traditions of their religion. Walking in downtown Durban, one might hear the voice of the *muezzin* (moo-EZ-in), the man who calls Muslims to prayer. His song is broadcast over a public address system from the central mosque, or place of worship.

Hindu women can be seen in the city wearing colorful silk saris. These are traditional long dresses made of draped cloth. From the Indian markets, the wonderful smell of incense, spices, and curries drifts into the streets.

White South Africans

Many white South Africans are Afrikaners. Afrikaners are descended mainly from Dutch settlers, but also from French and German immigrants. The Afrikaners created apartheid and held most of the important government positions. They controlled the country's agriculture during the apartheid years. Most Afrikaners belong to the Dutch Reformed church. They speak the language Afrikaans.

There is also a big group of white South Africans that can trace their ancestry back to a wave of British settlers in 1820. Most English-speaking South Africans are Christians. They belong to churches such as the Anglican (similar to the Episcopal church in the United States) and Methodist. A small group belongs to the Catholic church.

There are also a number of whites whose first language is English but who did not come from Britain. For example, many Russian Jews and other European Jews came to South Africa hoping to escape religious persecution in the early 1900s. They wanted to find a safe home in a place full of opportunities.

These people settled in the towns that were springing up around the goldfields. Today, there are about 130,000 Jewish people in South Africa. They have contributed a great deal to South Africa's economic, educational, and cultural life.

There are about 750,000 South Africans of Portuguese ancestry. Many of their ancestors came from Portugal. Others came from the Portuguese colonies of Angola and Mozambique, South Africa's neighbors to the north, after Portugal withdrew from those colonies. Many of these people are highly skilled farmers and work in the fruit and vegetable trade. They speak Portuguese and a variety of African languages.

Bustling Cities, Quiet Villages

South African cities are very modern, with sprawling highways, tall glass-and-steel buildings, and large shopping malls. There is, however, a big gap between rich and poor. Most urban blacks live in poor townships on the outskirts of the city.

Skyscrapers and other large buildings make up the Durban skyline.

Most whites live in attractive, clean suburbs. Most of the rich people are educated whites, while most of the poor people are unskilled blacks who have low-paying jobs in factories or work as domestic servants. Now that apartheid is over, people are hopeful that life will improve for the black population.

Johannesburg is the largest city in South Africa. At first, it grew because of the gold mines in the area. The downtown region bustles during the day but is quiet at night. One reason is that most people go home at the end of the workday. Another reason is fear of street crime. Since there is high unemployment and much poverty, crime is common.

South Africa's other major cities are smaller, but they still have a big-city feel. Durban is a large, busy port city on the east coast of South Africa. Ships from all over the world stop at its

harbor. There are many factories in Durban's industrial area. And tourists flock to Durban's luxurious beachfront hotels to enjoy the year-round warm weather.

Cape Town, the oldest settlement in South Africa, is a beautiful city. It lies at the foot of Table Mountain. Cape Town is the country's legislative, or law-making, capital. Pretoria, in the northern part of the country, is the government's administrative capital, which sees that laws are put into effect. Pretoria is known for its lovely jacaranda tree–lined streets. Bloemfontein, in the center of the country, is South Africa's judicial capital—the branch of government that interprets, or explains, the laws and decides cases. The southeastern coastal city of Port Elizabeth, the center of the automobile industry, is very important to the country's economy.

The first settlers were drawn to the beautiful coastline around Cape Town.

SAY IT IN ZULU AND AFRIKAANS

Here is how you would say some common words and phrases in Zulu and in Afrikaans:

English	Zulu	Afrikaans
Hello	Sabona (sah-BOH-nah)	Hallo
How are you?	Sapele kunjani?(sah-PEE-leh koon-JAH-nee)	Hoegaandit? (hoo-CHAHND-it)
Yes	Yebo (YEAH-baw)	Ja (YAH)
No	Cha (TCHA)	Nee (KNEE-uh)
Please	Ngiyancenga (ngee-yan-KSENG GAH)	Asseblief (us-ah-BLEEF)
Thank you	Ngiyabonga (ngee-yah-BONG-AH)	Dankie (DUNN-key)
I'm sorry	Ngixolele (Ngee-koh-LEH-LEH)	Ek is jammer (EHK iss YUM-mer)
What's your name?	Ubani Igama (OO-BAH-neel GAH-ma)	Wat is jou naam? (vut iss yo NAHM?)
Good-bye	Sale kahle (salla GAHSH-leh)	Totsiens (TOT-seens)

Life in South Africa's countryside is not necessarily quiet and slow. In some parts of the country, you can find an unhurried way of life that has been passed down from one generation to the next. But in other parts, you find high technology at work, with the latest combine harvesters and modern irrigation methods in use. Most of the land—more than 85 percent—however, isn't suitable for large-scale commercial farming. There simply is not enough rain.

The main crops in South Africa are corn—a staple, or important, food of the black population—wheat, sugarcane, and fruit. Vineyards for growing grapes to make wine are an important part of the country's agriculture and were introduced by French settlers. South Africa also has some large cattle and sheep ranches. Wool is one of the leading exports.

Most of the large farms are owned by whites, while the farm laborers are black. Blacks who have their own farms usually have poorer quality soil. They usually can grow only enough food to feed their families. This is called subsistence farming. It is an extremely hard way of life. Often the men leave these farms, which are scattered throughout the country, to try to find work in the cities. The women, young children, and the elderly are left to try to coax some crops from the soil.

Leopard Skins and Tennis Shoes

The clothes that the people of South Africa wear today are a mixture of traditional and modern. They are also a mixture of African and Western (European and North American).

Walking down a street in Johannesburg, one might see a man wearing blue jeans, a T-shirt, and American-style running shoes.

A woman from a rural village might be wearing an African headdress made of cloth, animal skin, and beadwork. Around her neck hang colorful beaded necklaces. While her skirt may be made of African batik fabric, her T-shirt and canvas sneakers are Western.

Men in T-shirts and hard hats carry Zulu shields.

29

An archway marks the entrance to a Zulu kraal, where beautifully decorated "beehive" huts are grouped together.

3
FAMILY LIFE, FESTIVALS, AND FOOD

Families,
Together and Apart

South Africa's many racial and ethnic groups speak different languages and have different customs, skin color, cultures, and religions. Yet they all share a love of family. They want their loved ones to enjoy all the good things that come with peace and prosperity. Most people wish for a comfortable home to live in, enough wholesome food to eat, nice clothes to wear, an education, medical care, and a good job.

Family and community are central to the African way of life. Villages and kraals—clusters of mud-brick houses or beehive-shaped huts—are usually built around a small fenced-in central area, where the cattle or goats are kept. Family members tend a nearby vegetable garden and a cornfield. Everyone helps. Grandmothers might watch toddlers, while ten-year-olds might help tend the animals.

Relatives are very important to one another in South Africa. Aunts and uncles are like extra sets of parents. Cousins are almost like brothers and sisters. But years of industrialization and apartheid have broken down this supportive

31

family system. In the early 1900s, life as black South Africans had known it changed. In order to make enough money, many men had to leave their villages to seek work. Those who found work as miners lived in hostels on the mine's property, sharing dormitories with hundreds of other men from around the country. They were far away from their wives and children. They were able to go home to visit just a few times a year. Those who found work in the cities were not permitted to bring their families with them. Some family members ignored the law and came to the city anyway, risking arrest and jail.

The city workers, who usually found jobs in factories or as unskilled laborers, moved into black townships on the outskirts of the cities. The townships quickly became known for their poverty and high crime rates. Still, a strong sense of family loyalty remained. This was true also among the black people who knew only city life and never had first-hand experience of the kraal.

Some breaks can never be mended. Apartheid forced families apart. But with the end of apartheid, the future looks brighter for the families of black South Africans.

Welcome Home

South Africans live in many different kinds of homes. In the countryside, black South Africans have used a variety of building materials and design styles. The traditional Zulu house is a grass hut shaped like a beehive. The floor is made of dirt, beaten smooth and then covered with a "cement" of dried cow dung. Another style of Zulu house is made of mud bricks. It is also round but has a thatched roof and is painted on the outside with beautiful, intricate patterns. The

Ndebele (en-duh-BEH-LEE) people also paint their houses with brightly colored geometric designs. These dwellings can be found in the rural areas that were once the homelands—parts of the country set aside under apartheid for black occupation. In these areas are also shanties. These are poor makeshift dwellings, built of thin sheets of metal, their roofs weighted down with bricks and rocks.

Outside the cities, the black townships contain rows and rows of boxlike houses. Each of these identical, four-roomed brick houses has a tiny yard. Residents pay rent to the government. In the large townships, such as Soweto, outside of Johannesburg, there are never enough homes available. The small houses there tend to be very overcrowded. Because of the housing shortage, unplanned, illegal shantytowns have also been built.

A woman wearing neck bands and a shawl walks in front of Ndebele houses decorated with colorful murals.

In addition to the townships and the shantytowns, another kind of shelter developed, called squatter camps. In the years before apartheid ended, some blacks felt they had to use violence to get what they needed. There were riots. Thousands were left homeless as property was destroyed. People flocked to safer areas, where they set up squatter camps. Anywhere that people could find some open land, usually close to a town, they would set up camp. They made shelters from cardboard, burlap sacks, and plastic sheeting. Entire settlements sprung up overnight because so many people were desperate for a place to live. This practice was dangerous because the squatters had no access to clean running water or toilet facilities. Disease could easily break out and spread.

In contrast, some of the most beautiful mansions in the world can also be found in South Africa. In Johannesburg's

A large shopping mall overshadows a hillside shantytown.

northern suburbs, there are expensive homes. Many have swimming pools, and some have private tennis courts. The biggest and best houses in every South African town can be found in the white, wealthy suburbs.

But not all white people are rich. There are many working-class neighborhoods. (They used to be all white but now are racially integrated.) These houses are fairly small with three bedrooms, one bathroom, a living room, and an eat-in-kitchen. Still, even these have separate servants' quarters in the backyard, left over from the past.

Now that apartheid is gone, the law does not restrict people to living in a certain area. One may live wherever one can afford a house. Very few nonwhites, however, can afford to live in expensive suburban homes. But apartment buildings in the cities are now multiracial.

Historical Holidays

With the recent change in government in South Africa came changes in some of the holidays the people celebrate. One had its name changed. The Day of Reconciliation, observed on December 16, used to be called the Day of the Vow. In 1838, a white Afrikaner named Piet Retief went with one hundred of his followers to see Zulu King Dingane. Retief wanted to make a treaty to get more land, but the Zulus ambushed and killed him and his group.

Other Afrikaners were angered by the news and wanted revenge on those who killed Retief. Andries Pretorius gathered together a number of soldiers. Before going to the Ncome River to attack the Zulus on December 16, they prayed for victory. They vowed that future Afrikaners would keep the day holy if they won. They did.

The December 16 holiday reminds people of the terrible conflicts between the races in South Africa. The new 1994 government thought it would help people begin to be less angry if the holiday were renamed. The word *reconciliation* means that people have come together to resolve their disagreements.

Another holiday that South Africans celebrate is Workers' Day. On May 1 of each year, workers rest and are recognized for their contributions to the nation.

Women's Day is celebrated on August 9. Youth Day is celebrated on June 16. Youth Day began after the riots in Soweto township in 1976. This was when black schoolchildren marched in peaceful protest against apartheid and police opened fire. Many children were killed or injured.

Religious Holidays

South Africans also observe various religious holidays. Christians of all races celebrate Christmas Day on December 25. Just before that day, streets and stores are decorated with pretty lights. People shop for gifts and go to parties. Since South Africa is in the Southern Hemisphere, Christmas falls in the middle of summer. Some people of European ancestry eat a feast of warm food, like a roast with all the trimmings, despite the hot weather. Most people, however, enjoy a barbecue in the backyard or go to the beach to swim and eat chilled watermelon. Some people go to church.

In South Africa many Christians observe a long Easter weekend, from Good Friday to Easter Monday. They also celebrate Easter Sunday, and many people attend church services. Shops, movie theaters, and other places may be closed for part of the long weekend. Government offices and schools are closed.

A Zulu Wedding Celebration

Among the Zulu, marriage arrangements are long and complicated. Gifts and messages go back and forth between the families. *Lobola* (la-BAWL-a), a bride price, is decided upon to make up for the "loss" of a daughter and to make sure that she is well treated in her marriage. Ten head of cattle is an average *lobola*, but sometimes more is paid by the groom's family, depending on the social importance of the bride's family.

Before the wedding, the bride-to-be braids her hair. (During her engagement, she wore it in a short topknot.) She puts on a traditional dress made of beads, while the groom wears animal skins. The ceremony is performed by the priest, or *induna* (in-DOO-nah), who is the representative of the king. An important purpose of the ceremony is to introduce the bride to her husband's deceased ancestors and to put her under their care.

Mbira (em-BEE-ra) music, with drums, song, and dance, is an important part of the celebration. A cow, or perhaps a goat, is killed, and the meat is slowly roasted for the wedding feast. *Ijuba* (ee-JOO-ba), a beer made from corn, is served. The festivities last through the early hours of the morning. A Zulu wedding is a combination of seriousness and fun. It is a celebration that involves the whole community.

Zulu warriors perform a ceremonial dance at a royal wedding.

Black members of churches that practice baptism meet from time to time outside, surrounded by nature. They may meet by a stream, in a stand of eucalyptus trees, or on a quiet beach. There, they sing, pray, and, wearing all their clothes, enter the water to purify themselves.

Jewish South Africans celebrate their New Year, called Rosh Hashanah, each September or October. The date changes according to the lunar calendar. They go to services at the synagogue (Jewish place of worship), then celebrate by eating apples dipped in honey. This symbolizes the hope for a good, sweet new year. Indian Hindus celebrate their New Year, called Diwali, in October or November. Indian Muslims keep to a fast from sunrise to sunset each day during the holy month of Ramadan. At the end of Ramadan, they end their fast by eating curries, samosas (fried dough with a curry filling), and sweet coconut treats.

Cultural Festivals

In addition to these historical and religious holidays, South Africans enjoy many cultural festivals. One is the Roodepoort Eistedfod (ROO-dah-PORT EYE-stett-FITT), a celebration of music, dance, and song. This takes place every other October. The dancers, musicians, and singers who perform at the festival are the best young amateurs in the country. The performers are of

Indian Muslims celebrate the 300th anniversary of Islam in South Africa with a parade.

many ages. Professional judges award points to the acts. Certificates are presented to the winners in a ceremony at the end of the festival.

Many tourists flock to the charming town of Knysna (NIZE-nah), along the Cape Garden route, for its summer festival. The main attraction is the region's seafood, including crayfish (like small lobsters), prawns (large shrimp), mussels, oysters, and a fish called kingklip. There are concerts of both classical and popular music, theater productions, and street performances.

A Zulu woman grinds corn by hand. She will use it to make beer.

Taste Treats

South Africa has excellent vegetables and meat products plus a variety of fresh seafood. There are Italian, Greek, French, Portuguese, and Chinese restaurants, as well as others that serve Indian and Southeast Asian dishes.

Corn, called *mealie*, is an important food among black South Africans in the countryside. *Mealie pap* is ground corn that is eaten as a porridge, mixed with curdled milk. When people get together for weddings or funerals, especially in rural areas, a cow or a sheep may be slaughtered. The meat is then cooked and served with *mealie pap*. Home-brewed beer is an important part of ceremonial occasions. Blacks who live in the cities also enjoy foods such as hamburgers, French fries, and sandwiches.

Afrikaners enjoy eating *boerewors* (boo-ree-VORS), a spicy sausage, at *braaivleis* (brah-FLASE), or barbecues. Steaks and chops are also grilled on the open fire at these cookouts. *Mealie pap* is often served as a side dish, complete with gravy.

Biltong (bil-TONG), which is like beef jerky, is a favorite South African snack. It was originally used by the Afrikaners because it would not spoil when they went on long trips. *Biltong* is made from strips of dried meat that has been salted and spiced. It is usually made from beef. For dessert, *koeksisters* (COOK-sisters) are a sweet and sticky treat. Lengths of pastry dough are braided, fried, and dipped in thick, sweet syrup.

Asian South Africans often use spices and curry powders in their cooking. An Indian curry meal will include several little bowls of condiments on the side, such as fruit chutney, dried coconut, sliced bananas, and raisins. Plain yogurt and cucumbers help to put out the "fire in your mouth" from a spicy curry. Kabobs, or *sosaties* (so-SAH-tees), are cubes of

SPICY YELLOW WALNUT RICE

2 cups rice	1 tablespoon salt
6 cups water	1 cup raisins or sultanas
3 tablespoons butter	1 tablespoon chopped walnuts
1 teaspoon turmeric	

Place the water in a saucepan and bring to a boil. Add all of the ingredients except the rice. Then add the rice slowly. Stir once. Cover the saucepan and simmer until the rice is tender and has absorbed all of the water—about 20 minutes. Stir and serve. The recipe makes enough for four to six people.

A street vendor sells a favorite treat of pineapple dipped in curry.

curried meat on a skewer. Between each cube there is a dried apricot or a piece of green pepper. Kabobs are served on a bed of yellow rice.

South Africans are becoming aware of the link between diet and health. Until fairly recently, most diets of South Africans were quite unhealthy—with too much animal fat being eaten and not enough whole grains, fruits, and vegetables. This is now beginning to change. Labels on some products now boast "low fat" or "no cholesterol." This is important because South Africans have a high rate of heart disease.

Supermarkets in South Africa are similar to those in the United States, except that there is not quite as much choice. Still, there is a big selection of fresh foods as well as canned goods and frozen foods.

On the streets of any town, one can find a number of food sellers. On simple wooden tables, they display brightly colored pyramids of fruits and vegetables. Others spread out their wares on blankets and newspapers. They sell potatoes, onions, peppers, grapes, oranges, and mangoes. Cooked corn on the cob or thick slices of pineapple dipped in curry and served on a wooden skewer can be bought and eaten right there in the street. This is the flavor of Africa!

Taking time out from school and work, a crowd watches as a street performer does his act.

4
SCHOOL AND RECREATION

Time for
Learning and Play

Under apartheid, there were separate public schools for each racial group—black, white, colored, and Asian. During that time, for every $12 spent on white education, approximately $6 was spent on Asian education, $4 on colored education, and just $1 on black education. This system made sure that whites would have better educations and so be able to hold on to their power. In the 1970s and the 1980s, black schoolchildren protested this unfair situation. These protests continued for years all across the country. Children boycotted the schools by refusing to attend classes. Some staged violent and destructive demonstrations, and sometimes school buildings were burned down.

Education is now racially integrated. Children may attend the school in their zoning area—this means either where the children live or where their parents work. Or, on a first-come, first-served basis, children may attend any school of their choice, if it has a space.

South Africa has some excellent colleges and universities. Under apartheid, they were also segregated, but sometimes a small number of nonwhites could attend white universities. Partial integration of the country's schools began at the university level. Often, this was the first time that people of different racial groups could meet as equals and have the opportunity to become friends.

Although all schools are integrated today, many problems remain. An entire generation of black children grew up with hardly any education. Now, as adults, they need jobs. But they have almost no opportunities because they have poor skills in reading, writing, and arithmetic.

The young children who are just starting kindergarten today should have a much brighter future. Children of all races can now sit side by side in their classrooms. Everyone hopes that South Africa will be a more peaceful place now that young people of all races are growing up together.

Classroom Classics

Education in South Africa is based on the British system. All children seven and older must attend school. Unlike public schools in North America, South African schools charge fees. Scholarships are available for those who cannot pay. These fees are now the same for everybody.

South African children have always worn school uniforms, and they are still required to do so today. Uniforms vary, but white shirts and blue blazers with the school's crest on the pocket are usually worn. Girls generally wear skirts, while boys wear long pants. Any children whose families cannot afford the uniforms are given a reduced rate or a scholarship to cover the cost.

Schoolgirls pose for a photo while on a field trip.

Children attend school for twelve years. Primary school covers about the same levels as first grade through seventh grade in North America. Seven-year-old children start school in what is called grade one, then go on to grade two. Third through seventh grades are called standards one through five. High school begins in standard six (eighth grade) in most places. Some schools divide this level into junior and senior high.

The school year begins in late January and ends in mid-December. Students have a week-long vacation in April, about three weeks in July (winter break), a week in October, and five weeks of summer vacation beginning in mid-December.

CAN YOU UNDERSTAND ZULU?

Hundreds of Zulu words were borrowed and adapted from English. Can you guess what these mean?

1. ibhaluni (EE-bah-LOO-nee)
2. ubhanana (OO-bah-NAH-nah)
3. ikhandlela (EE-kun-DLEH-LAH)
4. ujusi (oo-JOO-see)
5. ithelefoni (EE-telleh-FAWN-ee)
6. ushokoledi (oo-shoh-koh-LAY-dee)
7. istrobheri (ee-STROH-BEH-ree)
8. ikhamera (EE-kumeh-RAH)
9. ifriji (ee-FREE-jee)
10. ithelevishini (ee-TELLEH-vee-SHEE-nee)

Answers: 1. balloon 2. banana 3. candle 4. juice 5. telephone 6. chocolate 7. strawberry 8. camera 9. refrigerator 10. television

In the last year of high school students take special examinations. The results of these exams determine if a student will be accepted by a college or university. Each region gives the same exams. Papers are graded by a special team of teachers for that area.

A new program has been started for students who get low grades on these exams. The program's goal is to help the students brush up on their skills. In this way, all students have a chance to go to college.

Do You Speak My Language?

In many ways, the new South African government is still figuring out what changes need to be made in the school system. Textbooks need to be rewritten to fill in accurate details of black history and apartheid. Before 1994, history textbooks

46

told a very one-sided story—that is, the history of the achievements of white South Africans only. Now, teachers, historians, and others are getting together to rewrite the textbooks so that a truer story of all South Africa's people will be told.

At the moment, most classes are taught in English. Recently, however, many classes have been taught in Afrikaans as well. Lately, there has also been some discussion about teaching in the "mother tongue"—the main language of an area where a school is located.

These friends enjoy cooling off at an outdoor slide.

Playtime

After school, most South African children enjoy playing outdoors. Schools offer all kinds of sports, and practices and matches are held most weekday afternoons. Tennis, swimming, rugby (a game similar to football but without the heavy equipment), cricket (a team game of British origin played with bat and ball), soccer, and netball are popular.

Many clubs have after-school meetings. Children can join their school's debate, drama, computer, or photography club, to mention just a few.

Surfers prepare to ride the waves on the coast of South Africa.

Young people enjoy a wide variety of other activities as well. Cities and towns have playgrounds, public parks, and swimming pools, in addition to libraries and museums. Young surfers in the coastal towns of Kwazulu-Natal have some of the world's best waves waiting for them after school. Watching television and going to the movies are rainy-day activities. As in many countries, the shopping mall is an ever-popular meeting place!

The Sporting Life

South Africans of all ages play a wide variety of sports. Both players and spectators are very enthusiastic. The country has had many famous athletes. South Africa has produced world-class tennis players such as Kevin Curran and Johan Kriek. Golfing greats Sally Little, Bobby Locke, and Gary Player are all from South Africa.

Beginning in the 1960s, South Africans were not allowed to participate in the Olympic Games and other international competitions. The other nations of the world were protesting South Africa's system of apartheid and hoped to pressure the nation to end the system. As apartheid was ended, one of the rewards for South Africans was being allowed back into the international sporting arena. The boycott ended in time for the 1992 Summer Olympic Games. Runner Elana Meyer won a silver medal in that year in Barcelona, Spain.

Rugby is the country's national sport. South Africa won the 1995 Rugby World Cup Championship. The victory brought the many different racial and ethnic groups together.

Cricket is played in the summer at most South African schools. The country has produced some excellent cricket teams. Soccer is also a much-loved game.

High school students in Johannesburg enjoy a game of soccer.

The South African group Ladysmith Black Mambazo performs for a crowd.

5
THE ARTS

Sounds of a
Cowhide Drum

South Africa has won much praise around the world for its theater. Plays are very popular because they provide people with both entertainment and a way to understand everyday life. And dramatic expression in South Africa has long been a form of protest against apartheid.

Actors John Kani and Winston Ntshona became well known for their work in protest theater. And as black South Africans began to feel freer to express themselves, more and more political plays were written. Groups of people began to work together on playwriting and production. The Market Theatre in Johannesburg put on several plays that went on to be performed in other countries. For example, the musical *Sarafina!* began at the Market Theatre before it went to Broadway in New York City and was then made into a movie starring the actress Whoopi Goldberg.

One of South Africa's most famous playwrights is Athol Fugard. Many of his plays have run for a long time in New

Black protest theater is one way that people have spoken out against injustice.

York City and other big cities. One, *Boesman and Lena*, is about a colored couple whose home is bulldozed to make way for a township.

Music

South Africa is famous for its wide variety of unique, beautiful music, both traditional and modern. The oldest African musical instrument is the human voice. From ancient times, black Africans have sung stories. In more recent times, Christian missionaries taught hymns to the blacks. Western harmonies influenced African rhythms. The choral style called *mbube* (em-BOO-bay) grew from these roots. It is performed around the world by the group Ladysmith Black Mambazo.

Traditional African instruments that are still played are drums, reed pipes, xylophones, and the *mbira* (em-BEE-ra)— an instrument made from a gourd, using metal strips that make sounds when tweaked. In the 1930s and 1940s, American jazz—which had its roots in Africa—now had a huge impact on music in South Africa. The new styles, known as *marabi* and *mbaqanga* (em-bah-KANG-gah), are sometimes called "township music."

Classical music is very popular in South Africa. The big cities have their own symphony orchestras. World-class opera productions also are staged. Afrikaner folk music, called *boeremusiek* (boor-eh-moo-SICK), is also very popular. It is similar to German and Austrian folk music, with the accordion as the most important instrument.

Music, played on a variety of instruments, is a big part of life in South Africa.

Dance

Ceremonial dances have been performed by South Africa's peoples for hundreds of years. There are Zulu dances that are performed for each special occasion. For example, there is a young warriors' dance and a wedding dance. Beadwork, skins, and shields are worn by the dancers, and ancient instruments are played.

The many different influences over the years have led to new kinds of African dances. One example is the gumboot dance of the miners. It is a kind of foot-stomping, boot-slapping dance performed by men. This dance was started by Zulu sugarcane workers on the coast and brought with them inland to the mining compounds.

In addition, South Africa offers classical ballet and modern dance performances—both amateur and professional.

Zulu children participate in a ceremonial dance.

Arts and Crafts

South Africa's ancient "rock art" is a national treasure. Cave paintings hundreds of years old show animals and how they were hunted. For centuries, Africans have also made beautiful stone sculptures and wood carvings.

Pottery, woodwork, basketwork, and beadwork are still created in much the same ways as they were centuries ago. Many of these fine crafts are now sought after by collectors.

The work of artists is usually influenced by events that

These handmade pots are used to hold corn beer.

happen in their lives. Both black and white South African artists have produced beautiful but disturbing paintings of township life and of barren homelands. Stunning photography comes out of both the harshness and beauty of South Africa. The photographs of Soweto township by Peter Magubane, for example, have been displayed all over the world.

Old Africa and the modern age meet in interesting ways. Today, some artists use traditional African designs for the borders of their computer-generated drawings. Clothing designers create outfits that blend African and Western styles. For example, denim jackets may have collars and cuffs embroidered with Zulu beadwork. Draped-cloth headdresses and matching caftans, or long loose dresses, of dyed batik fabric have become high fashion.

The Power of Words

South African literature is written mostly in English, although there are several excellent writers in Afrikaans, too. The country's history and politics have provided a wealth of material. The publication in 1948 of Alan Paton's novel *Cry the Beloved Country* was especially important. Its story has to do with the conflicts, fears, and prejudices of South Africans. Paton's book forced South African readers to look at what was happening around them—and to question it. For its readers in other countries, the novel revealed the truth of the South African tragedy. In 1995, *Cry the Beloved Country* was made into a movie.

Novelist and short-story writer Nadine Gordimer won the Nobel Prize for Literature in 1991. She writes about apartheid and the changes that have been made since the system was ended.

Up until the last few years of apartheid, there was strict censorship in South Africa. Antigovernment literature was often banned. Some writers, such as Breyten Breytenbach and the poet Jeremy Cronin, were imprisoned. There was a lot of "protest art," however, in spite of the dangers.

Nadine Gordimer

In the 1970s, much black poetry was written. Oswald Mtshali's first published collection was called *Sounds of a Cowhide Drum*. It was published by a small company. The poets Sipho Sepamla and Wally Mongane Serote were also published in this way. But some of South Africa's best black writers, including Dennis Brutus and Sepamla, left the country for fear of going to prison. Some have returned to South Africa now that apartheid is over.

56

SOUTH AFRICA IN ARTS AND LETTERS

Gerard Sekoto (seh-KOH-toh) (1913–   ), sometimes called the father of contemporary black South African art, works in watercolors, oils, and charcoal. He left South Africa in 1947 and has lived in Paris, France, ever since.

Nadine Gordimer (1923–), an internationally acclaimed author of short stories and novels, is a white South African. She was controversial in her own country for many years because of her strong opposition to apartheid. She writes about complex human relationships and the impact of politics. She won the 1991 Nobel Prize for Literature.

Athol Fugard (1932–   ) is South Africa's best-known playwright. Many of his plays are about tensions between blacks and whites.

Hugh Masekela (muss-uh-KEH-la) (1939–   ) is a world-famous trumpet player and jazz musician. He left South Africa in search of greater freedom, acceptance, and opportunity. His 1968 song "Grazin' in the Grass" sold 4 million copies. He co-wrote the music to the 1987 stage production of *Sarafina!* During his years in exile, he often toured and recorded with renowned South African singer **Miriam Makeba** (mah-KEH-ba). She is famous for her rendition of the Xhosa "click" song and, among black South Africans, for her outspoken opposition to apartheid.

Oswald Joseph Mtshali (em-CHAH-lee) (1940–   ) is a poet whose work has attracted wide attention. He has been published in South Africa as well as in Britain and the United States.

In the last few years, a number of South African writers and artists of children's books have made black children the main characters in their stories. These books show black children that they are important enough to have books written about themselves. They also help white children get an idea of a black child's life. The demand for children's books like these is growing in a country that seeks to break down racial barriers. This is just one of the exciting changes that are occurring as South Africans explore their newfound freedoms and travel the road to equality.

Country Facts

Official Name: Republeck van Suid-Afrika (Republic of South Africa)

Capital: Pretoria

Location: at the southern most tip of Africa, bordered on the north by Namibia, Botswana, and Zimbabwe. On the east lie Swaziland, Mozambique, and the Indian Ocean; and on the south and west lies the Atlantic Ocean.

Area: 471,444 square miles (1,221,040 square kilometers). *Greatest distances:* east–west: 1,010 miles (1,625 kilometers); north–south: 875 miles (1,408 kilometers). *Coastline:* 1,791 miles (2,881 kilometers)

Elevation: *Highest:* Giant's Castle, 10,868 feet (3,314 meters). *Lowest:* sea level at the coast

Climate: moderate throughout most of the country year-round; rainfall mostly in the summer

Population: 45,095,459

Form of Government: republic

Important Products: *Agriculture:* corn, milk, tobacco, potatoes, wheat, sugarcane, fruit, and wool. *Manufactured goods:* clothing, processed food, chemicals, plastics, and machinery. *Natural resources:* gold, diamonds, iron, coal, copper, chromium, platinum, uranium, limestone, and manganese

Basic Unit of Money: rand; 1 rand = 100 cents

Languages: There are eleven main languages. They are English, Afrikaans, Zulu, South and North Sotho, Tswana, Pedi, Tsonga, Ndebele, Xhosa, Swazi, and Venda

Religion: Christian; Hindu; Muslim; Jewish; and traditional African religions

Flag: The South African flag is shaped like a Y on its side and has stripes of black, yellow, red, green, white, and blue

National Anthem: *Nkosi Sikelel' i Afrika* ("God Bless Africa")

Major Holidays: New Year's Day, January 1; Good Friday and Easter Monday; Constitution Day, April 27; Workers' Day, May 1; Youth Day, June 16; Women's Day, August 9; National Heritage Day, September 21; Day of Reconciliation, December 16; Christmas Day, December 25

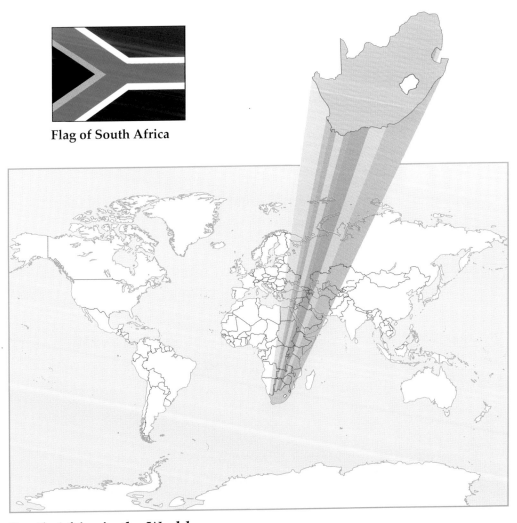

Flag of South Africa

South Africa in the World

Glossary

Afrikaans: the language spoken by Afrikaners, similar to old Dutch and Flemish

Afrikaner: a white South African of mainly Dutch descent

apartheid (uh-PAR- tate): an Afrikaans word for "separateness"; the system of government that separated the races in South Africa from 1948 to 1994

batik: a hand-printed fabric

Boer (BOOR): an Afrikaans word for "farmer," it refers to the early Afrikaners

colored: the term that was used during apartheid to describe people of mixed race

homelands: parts of the country that were set aside for black Africans during the period of apartheid

industrialization: the process whereby machinery comes to be used to do the work once done by people

kraal (CRAWL): a cluster of huts surrounding a pen for cattle

lobola (la-BAWL-a): bride price, or dowry; the money or goods paid by the groom's family to the bride's family

mbira (em-BEE-ra): a musical instrument made from a gourd, using metal strips that make sounds when tweaked; also called a thumb piano *muezzin* (moo-EZ-in): the man who calls Muslims to daily prayer

polygamy: the custom in some cultures in which a man has more than one wife at the same time

rural: referring to the countryside

shanties: makeshift shelters usually made of thin sheets of metal

trekboers (TREK-boors): Boers who traveled by oxen-drawn wagons into the interior of South Africa to escape British control in the 1800s

urban: referring to the city

veld: a grassland, usually having scattered shrubs

Western: refers to ideas and practices that come from Europe and present-day North America

For Further Reading

Dell, Pamela. *Nelson Mandela: Freedom for South Africa*. Chicago: Childrens Press, 1994.

Jacobsen, Karen. *South Africa*. Chicago: Childrens Press, 1989.

Meisel, Jacqueline Drobis. *South Africa at the Crossroads*. Brookfield, CT: Millbrook Press, 1994.

Paton, Jonathan. *The Land and People of South Africa*. New York: J. B. Lippincott, 1990.

Rosmarin, Ike. *Cultures of the World: South Africa*. New York: Marshall Cavendish, 1993.

South Africa in Pictures. Minneapolis, MN: Lerner Publications Company, 1988.

Steub, Conrad. *Enchantment of the World: South Africa*. Chicago: Childrens Press, 1986.

Index

Page numbers for illustrations are in boldface

About the Author

Jacqueline Drobis Meisel was born in the small gold-mining town of Welkom in the Orange Free State province of South Africa. She attended St. Andrew's Primary School, which was the only school in the area for English-speaking white children. By the time she left Welkom with her family at the age of eleven, she was strongly aware of her country's unfair racial laws.

Ms. Meisel attended high school in the bustling port city of Durban. She had some excellent teachers who made social studies and English literature come alive in the classroom. They encouraged her to read a wide variety of books and to keep a journal of her observations and ideas.

Ms. Meisel graduated from the University of the Witwatersrand in Johannesburg and went on to teach high school for two years. She hoped to inspire her students the same way that her remarkable teachers had inspired her. By that time, however, the problems in South Africa had become so severe that she made the difficult decision to leave the country. She now lives in California with her husband, Alex, and their two sons. She has returned, though, to her native land to research material for articles and books. In 1994, she wrote a book for young adults about the first free elections in her home country, entitled *South Africa at the Crossroads*.